Passages

volume 1:
Finding Wisdom

m.press is a small, spiritually-focused imprint of White Bison Publishers dedicated to bringing a unique self-discovery into everyday life through the wisdom contained within ancient scriptures.

Scripture taken from the New Century Version®. Copyright © 2005 by Thomas Nelson, Inc. Used by permission. All rights reserved.

Scripture taken from The Voice™. Copyright © 2012 by Ecclesia Bible Society. Used by permission. All rights reserved.

Scripture quotations marked (CEV) are from the Contemporary English Version Copyright © 1991, 1992, 1995 by American Bible Society, Used by Permission.

Scripture quotations marked (NLT) are taken from the Holy Bible, New Living Translation, copyright ©1996, 2004, 2015 by Tyndale House Foundation. Used by permission of Tyndale House Publishers, Inc., Carol Stream, Illinois 60188. All rights reserved.

Topical structure adapted from International Students, Inc. The ancient texts are based on the earliest and best manuscripts from the original languages (Greek, Hebrew, and Aramaic). The story-based passages collectively help the reader imagine a new way to live, achieve clarity in understanding, and find insights for personal application.

Passages in this series are repeated, either in the same translation or in a different translation. As you look again at a passage you have already read and considered, let the new topic build on your previous thoughts. Even when the story is already familiar, you can discover new insights and find new applications to enrich your experience.

The included texts use a common chapter and verse system. Each is divided into chapters and further divided into verses. The reference for a particular verse includes the book name, followed by a chapter number, a colon or a period, then the verse number. When reading the passages in this book, including the chapter or verse numbers is not necessary, and is not recommended.

The methodology encouraged for study of the wisdom contained in this book is the *Discovery* approach or individual meditation.

The artwork and book design was created by [ten thousand one] & developed by roberts & co. and is copyrighted material ©2019, by m.press, ltd. and [ten thousand one].

PRINT ISBN:
978-1691107469

ISBN 10:
1691107468

To learn more about *m.press* or
its organization please visit:
www.AncientPassages.org

or to connect to our founder Larry Hargrave please reach out at www.larryhargrave.com.

Our Thoughts:

These passages are designed to be meditated on with the topics mentioned in mind. This can be done alone or with a small group. We encourage you to utilize the "Discovery" approach when reading these ancient stories. It's a unique way to get out of the way and let God speak to us through scripture.

What you may find could be miraculous...

Dedication

The richness of the timeless, ancient stories, the way they dig into you as you dig into them, will amaze you and challenge you to be more, so you can do more. This happens whether you are reading alone, with another person, or in community with others who are also seeking wisdom.

The process is simple. The tools are practical. The approach is proven. The passages are powerful.

This collection did not happen accidentally. It was the purpose and plan of numbers of determined individuals. It has become the experience of millions of individuals in groups worldwide, and yet, apart from this topical series, it is unlikely you have ever encountered it, or even heard of it. It is the goal of our team and our partners to change that for you, and for others in your circle of influence — those you care about: friends, family, coworkers, and those who just happen to cross your path.

Our friend and mentor, John King, challenged us and offered us the opportunity to take what has been made openly available in other ways, and give it a print and digital home. This work is dedicated to John, to those like him who have birthed and nurtured the "how to's", and to countless individuals who are dedicated to seeing Wisdom and Peace awakened in their own lives, and in the lives of others.

Table of Contents

Preface	8
Optional Guidelines	21
I.　*Creation to the Messiah/Christ*	27
God creates all things	28
people disobey God & God's response	33
God's special promise	37
the blessing of forgiveness	39
God's suffering servant	42
the birth of Jesus	45
II.　*Jesus and You*	49
Jesus meets a man seeking God	50
Jesus calms a storm	53
Jesus' authority over death	55
Jesus dies on a cross	60
Jesus rises from the dead	64
becoming a child of God	67
III.　*Jesus' Life*	70
Jesus is baptized	71
the testing of Jesus	74
Jesus meets the Samaritan woman	78
Jesus' authority over spirits	82
death and burial of Jesus	85
Jesus meets followers after rising again	88

Table of Contents

IV. *God Makes a Way*	92
God creates people	93
God judges his creation	96
God makes promises to all creation	100
Abraham's big test	103
God's commands	106
God's Word makes us wise	110
V. *Jesus is the Way*	112
man's special relationship with God	113
all have turned away from God	116
sacrifices for sin	119
how we will know the Messiah/Christ	123
Jesus heals a paralyzed man	125
Jesus shares a last meal	128
VI. *Finding Wisdom*	131
to overcome temptation	132
to find and show love	135
to not fear circumstances	139
to forgive and restore	141
to keep unity in Christ	144
to gain wisdom for living	146

a Preface by our Founder

When we landed I stepped out into what I expected, a third world country, one of the poorest. What I was not prepared for, in a very dark night, was the pressing humanity — thousands of people in the dark shadows, constant shouting, motorcycles revving to a high-pitched scream, and racing threateningly among the throngs of people.

The humidity slapped me in the face and the smells were somewhere between stale and a stench. We were escorted to and from customs by a petite Sargent wearing a large gun on her right hip. The gun looked even larger on her. Our luggage was brought into a rope-fenced area that was lit by a floodlight run by a smoking generator. Immediately men stepped from the darkness into the edge of the light around the fence. I learned later they were part of the Sargent's security team.

We needed a bathroom. In her acquired British accent she explained that she could not secure our safety in the darkened outside public restroom area. Instead she led us to her house about a block and a half away from our luggage. She wanted all of us inside. She lived in a stand-alone building about the size of a standard American garage. There was an animal skin rug on the rock floor beside a bed, a small table, a lamp, and an open pantry with some canned goods in it. That wasn't the only thing that was open. The toilet was just sitting in the room. There was a small sink with running water. We were told we would need to put water in the tea kettle and pour it into the toilet to flush. She turned away toward the door.

I could now see her face in the light. She had a determined look about her. She was beautiful and the scar across one cheek did not mar her beauty. I asked her if she had lived in her home long and she answered that when she was promoted to lead the airport security teams she had been given this place to live, always near her work, and she was privileged to have a place to herself. As I took my turn at the toilet, her soft conversational tone changed to a commanding voice as she spoke loud enough for everyone to hear, "Finish what you have to do, but I have orders to keep you moving."

Our travel gear had been moved into the back of two vans and the security team, a ragged looking group of men in street clothes, very different from the smartly dressed Sargent, were standing by. They were intimidating, looking intently out into the darkness, and it occurred to me that they were probably battle-hardened from the horrors of the latest war, a war that devastated the entire country.

As the vans pulled away, the Sargent held up her left hand and waved slightly. I thought she was looking at me. We went through narrow streets and finally onto a version of a blacktop highway. As our driver sped away I checked my watch. Most of us had been traveling for 15 to 18 hours and we had a four-hour drive ahead of us.

As we sped along I estimated our van's stopping distance to be well beyond where the driver could first see even a reflector in the driving rain and total darkness.

There was another problem. There were no reflectors. I was wondering why our driver was driving in the middle of the road. The answer came quickly. A large black truck that was stopped in our lane materialized out of the fog, rain, and darkness. There was no warning, no lights, no reflectors, nothing. Our driver swerved hard and never had time to even touch his brakes. I don't know how we cleared the truck, but our troubles weren't over. As the van shook and swayed, we were tossed about. When we were back in the middle of the road I saw the second van had also cleared the truck. The driver of the second van began flashing his low and high beams and our driver pulled over and stopped.

I saw the second driver in the side mirror as he ran up, pulled our driver out of the van and began screaming at him as they pushed each other back and forth on the asphalt. Finally, our driver dropped back and the second driver continued to scream at him. One of the men with us had lived in the region where we were going, and he explained that the second driver was telling our driver to slow down, that he could kill himself if he wanted to, but he was not to endanger us.

When we pulled out our driver reduced his speed for a few kilometers, and then increased his speed again. I turned to the man who had spoken and whispered just above the noise of the van, "Say something to him." The man whispered back, "He is obviously a good driver. I think we should take our chances with that and not rile him again." I nodded, and we continued our drive in the darkness.

I was still awake when we pulled off the highway onto some rough roads. It was just before 4am when we arrived at a compound. As they were opening the gate, our trip coordinator came from the second van to explain that these were the best available accommodations. Our housing for the next several days would not be available until the next night. We would each have a room, and we were to be packed and loaded before breakfast at 7am.

The best accommodations looked like a previously bombed-out reconstruction that had never been completely rebuilt. The generator was off for the night. The only light was from our LED headlights. After three hours of trying to sleep we grabbed some fruit, bread, and instant coffee.

Our time that day and much of our time over the next days was spent going to various villages. We would be ceremonially welcomed and offered rice cooked with a vegetable, and sometimes a meat or fish. Some of us were initially cautious in eating the food, but we all learned quickly to eat only a small portion and generously thank the people who had prepared it. That simple meal was an extravagance prepared for us, but whatever food was left was all these people would have to eat that day.

It was in the villages that we saw peace reining between people of conflicting faiths and factions. We met men and women of influence who had opened the door for discovery studies to be started and accepted in their villages and we heard their stories. These people were always individually introduced to us as a 'Man or Woman of Peace.' The introductions were lengthy, and everyone applauded as they were being introduced. There was an evident pride on their part as they stood in their formal and colorful clothing to be acknowledged.

We observed the groups each time reading an ancient passage, asking the same simple questions, and following a pattern of guidelines that could easily and rapidly be reproduced in other groups. It was explained to us that there were no leaders in the groups. Everyone took turns asking the questions. No one ever told anyone else in a group what to think, what to believe, or what to do. Each person either discovered for themselves from the passage or from the discoveries shared by others in the group. We had been told that the groups build a greater sense of community and accountability. We saw both and sensed that was happening. We were there when a group of one faith opened their meeting area (a concrete platform in the center of the village) to be used by a group from another faith.

We saw people of great joy who were living in the midst of great hardship and caring for others without prejudice — others who did not share, or no longer shared their traditions, and no longer worshipped their god or their gods.

We did things that were very different from our world, like walking across a narrow, jagged bamboo bridge with no side rails, crawling at times to maintain our balance, with continuous warnings from our interpreters to not fall from the bridge to the crocodiles in the water below.

We saw schools that had been built by one faith for the children of another faith. We saw water wells that had been dug by one faith for the use of another faith. We heard the stories of one faith putting their bodies and their lives between attacking members of their own faith to protect the lives of another faith. We saw rice, cooking oil, and medical supplies being stockpiled at great sacrifice by one faith to save and sustain the lives of another faith in what would quickly become a devastating national disaster.

We saw what we no longer or very rarely see in our own countries: a belonging to each other, people serving the best interest of others that superseded the descent and differences that had dominated previous generations for centuries. We saw hope and support for diverse people in one of the most unlikely places on the planet. I began to wonder if this could happen in our home countries, and, if so, how?

After that first short night we were staying in a two-story brick building in an open compound on a hill in the city. I later accidentally discovered that we had displaced families who normally lived where we were staying, and they were living communally on mats in a large covered concrete area. I was given a larger room on the second floor. From the window I could see the shed where the generator was housed, the open area where the women cooked our meals, and the trail that led down to the well. Water was carried up to the compound.

On the first night all of us were exhausted. I inflated the rolled up sleeping pad I had brought, and laid it over an ultra-thin mattress supported by rough hand-hewn bed slats. At 3am I woke up and went over to the window. The rain was coming down in dense sheets, more like a waterfall than what I had ever experienced in a rainstorm. It was difficult to see the generator shed, but when lighting flashed I could see a shadowy figure standing under the eve of the building and looking out to the trail and the open area behind the building.

The torrential rain was pouring from the brim of his hat and I wondered how he could see anything, but he was there. It occurred to me that he was there to guard the generator, but I learned later that there were several night guards stationed around our building.

The population was dense in the city. Many more people lived there, but most lived much like the villagers. In the late evening the smoke from a myriad of open cooking fires could be seen on the mountainside across a valley. The traffic was insane and intense. None of us could figure out the rules, if there were rules, and we all agreed that none of us would have survived driving ourselves.

Our breakfast before we went out in the morning was mostly fruit and some kind of porridge with Nescafé instant coffee packets. Maybe because it was the only coffee available, but I started really liking the coffee before we left. We were assured the fruit was carefully washed in good water and all of the water we consumed was bottled. Contrary to stories we had heard, no one got sick. The days were long. Lunch would be very little in a village, and dinner was later after we returned. The dinner meals were very good and always included chicken.

One morning before breakfast I went outside with my Nescafé. There were two chairs under a tree and Gary Jennings was already sitting in one of the chairs with his coffee. A pesky, aggressive rooster was pacing around the chairs crowing continually. As I sat down, I looked at the rooster, and said, "What about this one?" Gary looked at him and said, "I hope he makes it to our dinner table tonight." I said I doubted if he would and we sat in silence for some moments except for the rooster who did not want us there.

Gary took a sip and looked up from his coffee. He was pensive as he said, "I did something this morning I have never done before. I often have some kind of reflective study or quiet time in the morning, but this morning I did a different kind of meditation. I took one of the passages they use in groups here and went through answering the questions with what I was thinking about and discovering for myself." I said, "I did the same thing for the first time and realized this approach is not just for groups." Gary then said what I was thinking. He asked, "How do we get this to happen in our home countries and communities?" I said, "I don't know yet." He said, "I don't either, but I am committing myself to help make it happen."

Some in our group chose to rest in the very few times when it was an option on the schedule, but Gary and I did not miss any of the larger meetings in the city. It was in these meetings that we saw with greater clarity how reading an ancient passage, asking eight simple questions, and following ten practical guidelines could make the discovery approach not only work in people's lives, but work powerfully to make peace among people who had previously hated and despised each other.

It was back in the two chairs under the tree with our coffee after dinner that we met again on the muggy, dark, overcast night before we would leave the country. A small light was still coming from the kitchen and with that and a single torch burning in the distance, we could see each other. Thankfully the rooster was not there protecting his territory.

We again asked ourselves what we could do to see peace-making movements also happen in our home countries and communities. We talked and realized we had some ideas, but we still didn't know the answers. Those moments were very emotional for both of us. We made commitments to each other to find answers and give ourselves to seeing the change they could bring about. That was several years ago. We have never wavered from our commitment or from encouraging each other.

This book is modeled after the individual and group study approach we observed. In it you can discover life-directing answers for yourself. People around you, either alone or in a group study, can discover answers for themselves — answers that will bring prevailing personal peace and greater wisdom.

What happened in small ways in villages, in surprising ways in our own meditations, and in bigger ways in the city can happen in you and in your world. The result can be a belonging to each other and serving the best interest of others that supersedes the descent and differences that have grown to dominate cultures. The result can be hope and support among diverse people even in most unlikely places.

Non-judgmental groups can become a place of support, where healing of hurts and care for the soul are not only possible, but present and pervasive.
Individuals can grow. Groups can be formed and can flourish with simple questions, practical guidelines, and ancient passages.

Each of us were impacted — changed. What we saw, we are beginning to see in our home countries!

Before we made the drive back to the airport, this time in daylight, we were taken to the city center. It was just a series of small, open shops where roads merged and the motorcyclists were very aggressive. At one point I was in the right place at the right time to grab one of our group and pull her onto a curb and away from a racing motorcycle that would have hit her. The cyclist never tried to stop. As he flew by, I realized there were unexpected dangers that even our shadowing guards, a police presence, or the soldiers stationed along our travel routes could not anticipate or prevent. I searched the faces around me and wondered who our guardians were. By now I was sure of one thing. They were always close.

People would step out from their makeshift shops and our guides would say something, sometimes in a voice that was stern, and then lead us to the shops of people they trusted. No one bought much, but the region was famous for the tie-dye technique artists use to produce vivid-colored fabrics for garments and home decor. We were taken to a shop where this was their specialty. I found three gifts to take home and several others bought gifts there, but the greatest gifts we would bring back were within us; what we had seen, what we had heard, and what we had experienced.

In the airport all of us were cleared through customs to leave the country except Gary. We never knew the reason, but he was being detained in a holding area. I called our hosts and decided to join Gary in the small room where he was sitting. I could not leave without him and I wanted to be with him. I was told that if I entered the room I would also be detained. As we sat in two chairs, the only furniture in the room, our flight time was nearing and nothing was happening. As Gary and I were being observed by security officers in the next room, I realized I had really begun to love this man, his heart, his compassion, his responses to what he had seen and experienced. At one point in our time together he said, "I will do anything for you, Larry." No one had ever said that to me.

I received a call from our hosts to let me know they had reached the Sargent and a government official. As I thanked them the Sargent and a smartly dressed man in a business suit came into the room. She smiled at me as she opened the door to the inner room and she and the man stepped inside. Something in my gut tightened and hurt as I thought about her and her world. I knew I would probably never see her again. As the man entered the room the guards snapped to attention. He walked past them to an office.

Within moments we were being hastily ushered without explanation and without apology out of the room, down the stairs past the customs area, out onto the tarmac, and up into the plane. Huge smiles from our team greeted us as we found our seats. We were all going to our homes. As I put my backpack away and settled in, going home felt good, but tears formed in my eyes. I was going home, but I was leaving a huge part of my heart behind in a place where life-changes were bringing about acceptance and peaceful culture changes. I was leaving with a deep desire to see what was happening there also happen in other places. I had never in such a short time begun to love people as I had in the villages and in the city. I was already feeling the precious pain of missing them that I thought might never go away. It never has.

As I write this, I am reminded of the two chairs under the tree, and the two chairs where Gary and I were detained. Our experience had more potential, and became more meaningful because we were in it together. I am also looking at an empty chair across from me. If you are up for adventure take a walk through the ancient passages, and see what you will discover. You could also find two chairs, ask someone to join you, and see what can happen together.

~Larry Hargrave

Recommendations:

You may select your topics separately, or go sequentially through the book, but before you begin, read and review the simple questions, the practical guidelines, and the discovery approach.

The questions, guidelines, and approach in this section are connection tools that enhance your experience with the passages, either in personal meditation, with another person, or in group study.

- The questions help determine a personal course of application and action.
- The guidelines aim to streamline and set sound practices in place for the discovery process.
- While following the approach is never mandatory or binding, it is a well-established path to engage in the passages with others.

There is more. Offering the passages and these recommendations as optional, self-selected topical discovery group studies within an organization introduces the potential for greater interpersonal team building and engagement. Goal setting and the achievement of those goals can be more consistent, more focused, and more attainable.

Simple Questions:

This is a process where individuals discover either by themselves or in a shared experience. The study sessions focus only on a current or previously covered passage (not other people's ideas, or outside content/sources). Everyone participates. One person asks the questions and runs the session. (Group members take turns doing this). No one in a group is to teach or add outside information into the study.

The following questions are asked and answered by individuals either in a personal meditation or a group session:

1. What happened last week for which you are thankful?

2. What challenge are you facing in your life, family, or community?

Review: How did you apply, tell and/or meet the need? Q. 6, 7, 8
(Not asked during the first session.)

3. Read the passage twice & re-tell the passage in your own words.

4. What did you (we) discover about God in this passage?

5. What did you (we) discover about people (humanity)?

6. How will you apply what you have discovered? (Start your answer with "I will".)

7. Will you tell the story of this passage to someone this week?

8. What can you (we) do to help with, or solve a challenge (#2)?

Practical Guidelines:

guidelines for a group

1. Avoid anyone talking too long.

2. Focus only on what this passage is saying *(not other passages)*.

3. Focus only on what this group is experiencing *(not other people's ideas, or outside sources)*. *[The question, "Where is that found in this passage?" helps avoid that.]*

4. Give people time to respond *(don't be afraid of silence, and allow people to "pass" if they so desire)*.

guidelines for the one running the session

5. Ask the questions. Don't teach. Don't lead. Encourage everyone to take turns being the one who runs the group.

6. Keep the session on schedule (one-hour max)— Complete all the questions. *(Note: This may be the hardest part.)* Encourage everyone to share.

7. Responding to questions from individuals — Ask, "What in this passage helps us answer your question?" Don't be too quick to contribute your answer/comment to the questions. Let the group respond and figure out their responses.

8. If an individual's question is not about the passage, say, "Let's discuss this further after our group time..." If it is a genuine question, the person will make time afterwards.

9. When dealing with "strange" or "wrong" interpretations or distracting questions/discussions, again, ask the question, "Where is that found in this passage?"

10. Close the group to new members joining when the group can be run by various group members and the group size exceeds 5-8 people. If a member wants to bring someone new after that, help them start a new group with that person and those that person can invite.

The Discovery Approach:

The discovery group studies approach is simple and straightforward. In the process with only passages, questions, and guidelines you can:

- Have an amazing ongoing personal experience of meditative discovery in the topics you choose.

- Sit down with a friend, neighbor, a family member or someone at work and do a discovery session with that one person. You can begin in any of the six sections or with any of the passages in this book.

- Start a group. This is a group of individuals you invite. After the group is established encourage those you have invited to explore finding and engaging with a person and encouraging that person to invite others into a new discovery group.

- When you ask a person to invite others to a group, you can initially meet with the new group; but there is a necessary and critical practice in the discovery group studies approach. If you <u>did</u> <u>not</u> invite the members of this new group, you will need to leave the group, and let it be run by its own members. When you refuse to do this or fail to do this, you will limit this new group's potential to multiply by starting other groups.

- Again, as difficult as this may be, you will no longer attend the new group. You can make yourself available to encourage anyone in the new group, but you must do it outside the group meetings.

Worldwide, individuals and groups of people are pursuing peace and greater wisdom in this process. They are discovering insights and gaining new understanding by combining simple questions and practical guidelines with what they find as they read ancient passages.

In the topical books in this series you are encouraged to explore something out of the ordinary that may offer a different take on life.

To learn more, to tell us your story, or to schedule a group coaching session in this simple, practical, and life-changing model, please visit:

www.AncientPassages.org.

Finding Ancient Wisdom for Discovery

section one

from creation to the Messiah/Christ

passage

God creates all things

Genesis 1:1-31

1 In the beginning God created the sky and the earth. 2 The earth was empty and had no form. Darkness covered the ocean, and God's Spirit was moving over the water. 3 Then God said, "Let there be light," and there was light. 4 God saw that the light was good, so he divided the light from the darkness.

5 God named the light "day" and the darkness "night." Evening passed, and morning came. This was the first day. 6 Then God said, "Let there be something to divide the water in two." 7 So God made the air and placed some of the water above the air and some below it. 8 God named the air "sky." Evening passed, and morning came. This was the second day.

9 Then God said, "Let the water under the sky be gathered together so the dry land will appear." And it happened. 10 God named the dry land "earth" and the water that was gathered together "seas." God saw that this was good.

11 Then God said, "Let the earth produce plants—some to make grain for seeds and others to make fruits with seeds in them. Every seed will produce more of its own kind of plant." And it happened.

12 The earth produced plants with grain for seeds and trees that made fruits with seeds in them. Each seed

grew its own kind of plant. God saw that all this was good. 13 Evening passed, and morning came. This was the third day.

14 Then God said, "Let there be lights in the sky to separate day from night. These lights will be used for signs, seasons, days, and years. 15 They will be in the sky to give light to the earth." And it happened.

16 So God made the two large lights. He made the brighter light to rule the day and made the smaller light to rule the night. He also made the stars. 17 God put all these in the sky to shine on the earth, 18 to rule over the day and over the night, and to separate the light from the darkness. God saw that all these things were good. 19 Evening passed, and morning came. This was the fourth day.

20 Then God said, "Let the water be filled with living things, and let birds fly in the air above the earth."

21 So God created the large sea animals and every living thing that moves in the sea. The sea is filled with these living things, with each one producing more of its own kind. He also made every bird that flies, and each bird produced more of its own kind. God saw that this was good. 22 God blessed them and said, "Have many young ones so that you may grow in number. Fill the water of the seas, and let the birds grow in number on the earth." 23 Evening passed, and morning came. This was the fifth day.

24 Then God said, "Let the earth be filled with animals, each producing more of its own kind. Let there be tame animals and small crawling animals and wild animals, and let each produce more of its kind." And it happened.

25 So God made the wild animals, the tame animals, and all the small crawling animals to produce more of their own kind. God saw that this was good.

26 Then God said, "Let us make human beings in our image and likeness. And let them rule over the fish in the sea and the birds in the sky, over the tame animals, over all the earth, and over all the small crawling animals on the earth."

27 So God created human beings in his image. In the image of God he created them. He created them male and female. 28 God blessed them and said, "Have many children and grow in number. Fill the earth and be its master. Rule over the fish in the sea and over the birds in the sky and over every living thing that moves on the earth."

29 God said, "Look, I have given you all the plants that have grain for seeds and all the trees whose fruits have seeds in them. They will be food for you.

30 I have given all the green plants as food for every wild animal, every bird of the air, and every small crawling animal." And it happened.

31 God looked at everything he had made, and it was very good. Evening passed, and morning came. This was the sixth day.[1]

---

[1] New Century Version (NCV)

passage

people disobey God

and God's response

Genesis 3:1-24

1 The snake was sneakier than any of the other wild animals that the Lord God had made. One day it came to the woman and asked, "Did God tell you not to eat fruit from any tree in the garden?" 2 The woman answered, "God said we could eat fruit from any tree in the garden, 3 except the one in the middle. He told us not to eat fruit from that tree or even to touch it. If we do, we will die." 4 "No, you won't!" the snake replied. 5 "God understands what will happen on the day you eat fruit from that tree. You will see what you have done, and you will know the difference between right and wrong, just as God does."

6 The woman stared at the fruit. It looked beautiful and tasty. She wanted the wisdom that it would give her, and she ate some of the fruit. Her husband was there with her, so she gave some to him, and he ate it too. 7 At once they saw what they had done, and they realized they were naked. Then they sewed fig leaves together to cover themselves. 8 Late in the afternoon, when the breeze began to blow, the man and woman heard the Lord God walking in the garden. So they hid behind some trees. 9 The Lord God called out to the man and asked, "Where are you?"

10 The man answered, "I was naked, and when I heard you walking through the garden, I was frightened and hid!" 11 "How did you know you were naked?" God asked. "Did you eat any fruit from that tree in the middle of the garden?" 12 "It was the woman you put here with me," the man said. "She gave me some of the fruit, and I ate it."

13 The Lord God then asked the woman, "What have you done?" "The snake tricked me," she answered, "and I ate some of that fruit." 14 So the Lord God said to the snake: "Because of what you have done, you will be the only animal to suffer this curse—For as long as you live, you will crawl on your stomach and eat dirt. 15 You and this woman will hate each other; your descendants and hers will always be enemies. One of hers will strike you on the head, and you will strike him on the heel."

16 Then the Lord God said to the woman, "You will suffer terribly when you give birth. But you will still desire your husband, and he will rule over you."

17 The Lord said to the man, "You listened to your wife and ate the fruit I told you not to eat. And so, the ground will be under a curse because of what you did. As long as you live, you will have to struggle to grow enough food. 18 Your food will be plants, but the ground will produce thorns and thistles.

19 You will sweat all your life to earn a living; you were made out of soil, and you will once again turn into soil."

20 The man Adam named his wife Eve because she would become the mother of all who live.

21 Then the Lord God made clothes out of animal skins for the man and his wife. 22 The Lord said, "They now know the difference between right and wrong, just as we do. But they must not be allowed to eat fruit from the tree that lets them live forever."

23 So the Lord God sent them out of the Garden of Eden, where they would have to work the ground from which the man had been made. 24 Then God put winged creatures at the entrance to the garden and a flaming, flashing sword to guard the way to the life-giving tree.[2]

---

[2] Contemporary English Version (CEV)

passage

God's special promise

Genesis 12:1-5

1 The Lord said to Abram, "Leave your country, your relatives, and your father's family, and go to the land I will show you.

2 I will make you a great nation,

and I will bless you.

I will make you famous,

and you will be a blessing to others.

3 I will bless those who bless you,

and I will place a curse on those who harm you.

And all the people on earth

will be blessed through you."

4 So Abram left Haran as the Lord had told him, and Lot went with him. At this time Abram was 75 years old. 5 He took his wife Sarai, his nephew Lot, and everything they owned, as well as all the servants they had gotten in Haran. They set out from Haran, planning to go to the land of Canaan, and in time they arrived there.[3]

---

[3] New Century Version (NCV)

passage

*the blessing
of forgiveness*

Psalm 32:1-11

1 Happy is the person whose sins are forgiven, whose wrongs are pardoned.

2 Happy is the person whom the Lord does not consider guilty and in whom there is nothing false.

3 When I kept things to myself, I felt weak deep inside me. I moaned all day long.

4 Day and night you punished me. My strength was gone as in the summer heat. *Selah*

5 Then I confessed my sins to you and didn't hide my guilt. I said, "I will confess my sins to the Lord," and you forgave my guilt. *Selah*

6 For this reason, all who obey you should pray to you while they still can. When troubles rise like a flood, they will not reach them.

7 You are my hiding place. You protect me from my troubles and fill me with songs of salvation. *Selah*

8 The Lord says, "I will make you wise and show you where to go. I will guide you and watch over you.

9 So don't be like a horse or donkey, that doesn't understand. They must be led with bits and reins, or they will not come near you."

10 Wicked people have many troubles, but the Lord's love surrounds those who trust him.

11 Good people, rejoice and be happy in the Lord. Sing all you whose hearts are right.[4]

---

[4] New Century Version (NCV)

passage

God's suffering servant

Isaiah 52:13 to 53:12

13 The LORD says: My servant will succeed! He will be given great praise and the highest honors. 14 Many were horrified at what happened to him. But everyone who saw him was even more horrified because he suffered until he no longer looked human.

15 My servant will make nations worthy to worship me; kings will be silent as they bow in wonder. They will see and think about things they have never seen or thought about before.

1 Has anyone believed us or seen the mighty power of the LORD in action?

2 Like a young plant or a root that sprouts in dry ground, the servant grew up obeying the LORD. He wasn't some handsome king. Nothing about the way he looked made him attractive to us.

3 He was hated and rejected; his life was filled with sorrow and terrible suffering. No one wanted to look at him. We despised him and said, "He is a nobody!"

4 He suffered and endured great pain for us, but we thought his suffering was punishment from God.

5 He was wounded and crushed because of our sins; by taking our punishment, he made us completely well. 6 All of us were like sheep that had wandered

off. We had each gone our own way, but the LORD gave him the punishment we deserved.

7 He was painfully abused, but he did not complain. He was silent like a lamb being led to the butcher, as quiet as a sheep having its wool cut off.

8 He was condemned to death without a fair trial. Who could have imagined what would happen to him? His life was taken away because of the sinful things my people had done.

9 He wasn't dishonest or violent, but he was buried in a tomb among cruel, rich people.

10 The LORD decided his servant would suffer as a sacrifice to take away the sin and guilt of others. Now the servant will live to see his own descendants. He did everything the LORD had planned.

11 By suffering, the servant will learn the true meaning of obeying the LORD. Although he is innocent, he will take the punishment for the sins of others, so that many of them will no longer be guilty.

12 The LORD will reward him with honor and power for sacrificing his life. Others thought he was a sinner, but he suffered for our sins and asked God to forgive us.[5]

---

[5] Contemporary English Version (CEV)

passage

the birth of Jesus

Luke 1:26-38; 2:1-20

26 During Elizabeth's sixth month of pregnancy, God sent the angel Gabriel to Nazareth, a town in Galilee, 27 to a virgin. She was engaged to marry a man named Joseph from the family of David. Her name was Mary.

28 The angel came to her and said, "Greetings! The Lord has blessed you and is with you." 29 But Mary was very startled by what the angel said and wondered what this greeting might mean.

30 The angel said to her, "Don't be afraid, Mary; God has shown you his grace. 31 Listen! You will become pregnant and give birth to a son, and you will name him Jesus. 32 He will be great and will be called the Son of the Most High. The Lord God will give him the throne of King David, his ancestor. 33 He will rule over the people of Jacob forever, and his kingdom will never end."

34 Mary said to the angel, "How will this happen since I am a virgin?" 35 The angel said to Mary, "The Holy Spirit will come upon you, and the power of the Most High will cover you. For this reason the baby will be holy and will be called the Son of God.

36 Now Elizabeth, your relative, is also pregnant with a son though she is very old. Everyone thought she

could not have a baby, but she has been pregnant for six months. 37 God can do anything!" 38 Mary said, "I am the servant of the Lord. Let this happen to me as you say!" Then the angel went away.

1 At that time, Augustus Caesar sent an order that all people in the countries under Roman rule must list their names in a register. 2 This was the first registration; it was taken while Quirinius was governor of Syria.

3 And all went to their own towns to be registered.

4 So Joseph left Nazareth, a town in Galilee, and went to the town of Bethlehem in Judea, known as the town of David. Joseph went there because he was from the family of David. 5 Joseph registered with Mary, to whom he was engaged and who was now pregnant.

6 While they were in Bethlehem, the time came for Mary to have the baby, 7 and she gave birth to her first son. Because there were no rooms left in the inn, she wrapped the baby with pieces of cloth and laid him in a feeding trough.

8 That night, some shepherds were in the fields nearby watching their sheep. 9 Then an angel of the Lord stood before them. The glory of the Lord was shining around them, and they became very frightened.

10 The angel said to them, "Do not be afraid. I am

bringing you good news that will be a great joy to all the people.

11 Today your Savior was born in the town of David. He is Christ, the Lord. 12 This is how you will know him: You will find a baby wrapped in pieces of cloth and lying in a feeding box. 13 Then a very large group of angels from heaven joined the first angel, praising God and saying:

14 "Give glory to God in heaven, and on earth let there be peace among the people who please God."

15 When the angels left them and went back to heaven, the shepherds said to each other, "Let's go to Bethlehem. Let's see this thing that has happened which the Lord has told us about."

16 So the shepherds went quickly and found Mary and Joseph and the baby, who was lying in a feeding trough. 17 When they had seen him, they told what the angels had said about this child. 18 Everyone was amazed at what the shepherds said to them.

19 But Mary treasured these things and continued to think about them. 20 Then the shepherds went back to their sheep, praising God and thanking him for everything they had seen and heard. It had been just as the angel had told them.[6]

---

[6] New Century Version (NCV)

Finding Ancient Wisdom for Discovery

section two
Jesus and You

passage

Jesus meets a man seeking God

John 3:1-21

1 There was a man named Nicodemus, a Jewish religious leader who was a Pharisee. 2 After dark one evening, he came to speak with Jesus. "Rabbi," he said, "we all know that God has sent you to teach us. Your miraculous signs are evidence that God is with you."

3 Jesus replied, "I tell you the truth, unless you are born again, you cannot see the Kingdom of God."

4 "What do you mean?" exclaimed Nicodemus. "How can an old man go back into his mother's womb and be born again?"

5 Jesus replied, "I assure you, no one can enter the Kingdom of God without being born of water and the Spirit. 6 Humans can reproduce only human life, but the Holy Spirit gives birth to spiritual life. 7 So don't be surprised when I say, 'You must be born again.'

8 The wind blows wherever it wants. Just as you can hear the wind but can't tell where it comes from or where it is going, so you can't explain how people are born of the Spirit."

9 "How are these things possible?" Nicodemus asked.

10 Jesus replied, "You are a respected Jewish teacher, and yet you don't understand these things? 11 I assure you, we tell you what we know and have seen, and yet you won't believe our testimony.

12 But if you don't believe me when I tell you about earthly things, how can you possibly believe if I tell you about heavenly things? 13 No one has ever gone to heaven and returned. But the Son of Man has come down from heaven. 14 And as Moses lifted up the bronze snake on a pole in the wilderness, so the Son of Man must be lifted up, 15 so that everyone who believes in him will have eternal life.

16 "For this is how God loved the world: He gave his one and only Son, so that everyone who believes in him will not perish but have eternal life. 17 God sent his Son into the world not to judge the world, but to save the world through him.

18 "There is no judgment against anyone who believes in him. But anyone who does not believe in him has already been judged for not believing in God's one and only Son. 19 And the judgment is based on this fact: God's light came into the world, but people loved the darkness more than the light, for their actions were evil. 20 All who do evil hate the light and refuse to go near it for fear their sins will be exposed. 21 But those who do what is right come to the light so others can see that they are doing what God wants.[7]

---

[7] New Living Translation (NLT)

passage

Jesus calms a storm

Mark 4:35-41

35 The same evening, Jesus suggested they cross over to the other side *of the lake*. 36 With Jesus already in the boat, they left the crowd behind and set sail along with a few other boats that followed. 37 *As they sailed,* a storm formed. *The winds whipped up* huge waves that broke over the bow, filling the boat *with so much water that even the experienced sailors among them were sure they were going to sink.* 38 Jesus was back in the stern of the boat, sound asleep on a cushion, when the disciples shook Him awake.

Disciples *(shouting over the storm)*: Jesus, Master, don't You care that we're going to die?

39 He got up, shouted words into the wind, and commanded the waves.

Jesus: That's enough! Be still! And immediately the wind died down to nothing, the waves stopped.

Jesus: 40 How can you be so afraid? *After all you've seen,* where is your faith? 41 The disciples were still afraid, *slowly coming to grips with what they had seen.*

Disciples *(to one another)*: Who is this *Jesus*? How can it be that He has power over even the wind and the waves? [8]

---

[8] The Voice

passage

Jesus' authority over death

John 11:1-44

1 There was a certain man who was very ill. He was known as Lazarus from Bethany, which is the hometown of Mary and her sister Martha. 2 Mary *did a beautiful thing for Jesus. She* anointed the Lord with a pleasant-smelling oil and wiped His feet with her hair. Her brother Lazarus became deathly ill, 3 so the sisters immediately sent a message to Jesus which said, "Lord, the one You love is very ill." 4 Jesus heard the message.

Jesus: His sickness will not end in his death but will bring great glory to God. As these events unfold, the Son of God will be exalted.

5 Jesus *dearly* loved Mary, Martha, and Lazarus. 6 However, after receiving this news, He waited two more days where He was.

Jesus *(speaking to the disciples)***:** 7 It is time to return to Judea.

Disciples: 8 Teacher, the last time You were there, some Jews attempted to execute You by crushing You with stones. Why would You go back?

Jesus: 9 There are 12 hours of daylight, correct? If anyone walks in the day, that person does not stumble because he or she sees the light of the world. 10 If anyone walks at night, he will trip and fall because he does not have the light within.

11 (Jesus briefly pauses.) Our friend Lazarus has gone to sleep, so I will go to awaken him.

Disciples: 12 Lord, if he is sleeping, then he will be all right. 13 Jesus used "sleep" *as a metaphor* for death, but the disciples took Him literally *and did not understand.*
14 Then Jesus spoke plainly.

Jesus: Lazarus is dead, 15 and I am grateful for your sakes that I was not there when he died. Now you will *see and* believe. Gather yourselves, and let's go to him.

Thomas, the Twin *(to the disciples)*: 16 Let's go so we can die with Him.

17-18 As Jesus was approaching Bethany (which is about two miles east of Jerusalem), He heard that Lazarus had been in the tomb four days.

19 Now many people had come to comfort Mary and Martha as they mourned the loss of their brother.

20 Martha went to meet Jesus when word arrived that He was approaching Bethany, but Mary stayed behind at the house.

Martha: 21 Lord, if You had been with us, my brother would not have died. 22 Even so I still believe that anything You ask of God will be done.

Jesus: 23 Your brother will rise to life.

Martha: 24 I know. He will rise again when everyone is resurrected on the last day.

Jesus: 25 I am the resurrection and the source of all life; those who believe in Me will live even in death.

26 Everyone who lives and believes in Me will never truly die. Do you believe this?

Martha: 27 Yes, Lord, I believe that You are the Anointed, *the Liberating King,* God's own Son who *we have heard* is coming into the world.

28 After this Martha ran home to Mary.

Martha *(whispering to Mary)*: Come with me. The Teacher is here, and He has asked for you.

29 Mary did not waste a minute. She got up and went 30 to the same spot where Martha had found Jesus outside the village. 31 The people gathered in her home offering support and comfort assumed she was going back to the tomb to cry and mourn, so they followed her. 32 Mary approached Jesus, saw Him, and fell at His feet.

Mary: Lord, if only You had been here, my brother would still be alive.

33 When Jesus saw Mary's *profound grief and the moaning and* weeping of her companions, He was deeply moved *by their pain* in His spirit and was intensely troubled.

Jesus: 34 Where have you laid his body? **Jews:** Come and see, Lord.

35 *As they walked,* Jesus wept; 36 and everyone noticed how much Jesus must have loved Lazarus.

37 But others were skeptical.

Others: If this man can give sight to the blind, He could have kept him from dying.

They are asking, if Jesus loves Lazarus so much, why didn't He get here much sooner?

38 Then Jesus, who was intensely troubled by all of this, approached the tomb—a *small* cave covered by a *massive* stone.

Jesus: 39 Remove the stone.

Martha: Lord, he has been dead four days; the stench will be unbearable.

Jesus: 40 Remember, I told you that if you believe, you will see the glory of God.

41 They removed the stone, and Jesus lifted His eyes toward heaven.

Jesus: Father, I am grateful that You have heard Me. 42 I know that You are always listening, but I proclaim it loudly so that everyone here will believe You have sent Me.

43 After these words, He called out in a thunderous voice.

Jesus: Lazarus, come out!

44 Then, the man who was dead walked out of his tomb bound from head to toe in a burial shroud.

Jesus: Untie him, and let him go.[9]

---

[9] The Voice

passage

Jesus dies on a cross

Luke 23:26-49

26 As Jesus was being led away, some soldiers grabbed hold of a man named Simon who was from Cyrene. He was coming in from the fields, but they put the cross on him and made him carry it behind Jesus.

27 A large crowd was following Jesus, and in the crowd a lot of women were crying and weeping for him. 28 Jesus turned to the women and said: Women of Jerusalem, don't cry for me! Cry for yourselves and for your children. 29 Someday people will say, "Women who never had children are really fortunate!" 30 At that time everyone will say to the mountains, "Fall on us!" They will say to the hills, "Hide us!" 31 If this can happen when the wood is green, what do you think will happen when it is dry?

32 Two criminals were led out to be put to death with Jesus. 33 When the soldiers came to the place called "The Skull," they nailed Jesus to a cross. They also nailed the two criminals to crosses, one on each side of Jesus.

34-35 Jesus said, "Father, forgive these people! They don't know what they're doing." While the crowd stood there watching Jesus, the soldiers gambled for his clothes. The leaders insulted him by saying,

"He saved others. Now he should save himself, if he really is God's chosen Messiah!"

36 The soldiers made fun of Jesus and brought him some wine. 37 They said, "If you are the king of the Jews, save yourself!" 38 Above him was a sign that said, "This is the King of the Jews."

39 One of the criminals hanging there also insulted Jesus by saying, "Aren't you the Messiah? Save yourself and save us!"

40 But the other criminal told the first one off, "Don't you fear God? Aren't you getting the same punishment as this man? 41 We got what was coming to us, but he didn't do anything wrong."

42 Then he said to Jesus, "Remember me when you come into power!"

43 Jesus replied, "I promise that today you will be with me in paradise."

44 Around noon the sky turned dark and stayed that way until the middle of the afternoon.

45 The sun stopped shining, and the curtain in the temple split down the middle. 46 Jesus shouted, "Father, I put myself in your hands!" Then he died.

47 When the Roman officer saw what had happened, he praised God and said, "Jesus must really have been a good man!"

48 A crowd had gathered to see the terrible sight. Then after they had seen it, they felt brokenhearted and went home.

49 All of Jesus' close friends and the women who had come with him from Galilee stood at a distance and watched.[10]

---

[10] Contemporary English Version (CEV)

passage

Jesus rises from the dead

Luke 23:50-24:12

50 Now there was a good and righteous man named Joseph. He was a member of the Jewish high council, 51 but he had not agreed with the decision and actions of the other religious leaders. He was from the town of Arimathea in Judea, and he was waiting for the Kingdom of God to come. 52 He went to Pilate and asked for Jesus' body. 53 Then he took the body down from the cross and wrapped it in a long sheet of linen cloth and laid it in a new tomb that had been carved out of rock. 54 This was done late on Friday afternoon, the day of preparation, as the Sabbath was about to begin.

55 As his body was taken away, the women from Galilee followed and saw the tomb where his body was placed. 56 Then they went home and prepared spices and ointments to anoint his body. But by the time they were finished the Sabbath had begun, so they rested as required by the law.

1 But very early on Sunday morning the women went to the tomb, taking the spices they had prepared.
2 They found that the stone had been rolled away from the entrance. 3 So they went in, but they didn't find the body of the Lord Jesus. 4 As they stood there puzzled, two men suddenly appeared to them,

clothed in dazzling robes.

5 The women were terrified and bowed with their faces to the ground. Then the men asked, "Why are you looking among the dead for someone who is alive? 6 He isn't here! He is risen from the dead! Remember what he told you back in Galilee, 7 that the Son of Man must be betrayed into the hands of sinful men and be crucified, and that he would rise again on the third day."

8 Then they remembered that he had said this.

9 So they rushed back from the tomb to tell his eleven disciples—and everyone else—what had happened.

10 It was Mary Magdalene, Joanna, Mary the mother of James, and several other women who told the apostles what had happened. 11 But the story sounded like nonsense to the men, so they didn't believe it.

12 However, Peter jumped up and ran to the tomb to look. Stooping, he peered in and saw the empty linen wrappings; then he went home again, wondering what had happened.[11]

---

[11] New Living Translation (NLT)

passage

becoming a child of God

John 1:1-18

1 In the beginning there was the Word. The Word was with God, and the Word was God. 2 He was with God in the beginning. 3 All things were made by him, and nothing was made without him. 4 In him there was life, and that life was the light of all people. 5 The Light shines in the darkness, and the darkness has not overpowered it.

6 There was a man named John who was sent by God. 7 He came to tell people the truth about the Light so that through him all people could hear about the Light and believe. 8 John was not the Light, but he came to tell people the truth about the Light.

9 The true Light that gives light to all was coming into the world!

10 The Word was in the world, and the world was made by him, but the world did not know him.

11 He came to the world that was his own, but his own people did not accept him. 12 But to all who did accept him and believe in him he gave the right to become children of God. 13 They did not become his children in any human way—by any human parents or human desire. They were born of God.

14 The Word became a human and lived among us. We saw his glory—the glory that belongs to the only

Son of the Father—and he was full of grace and truth.

15 John tells the truth about him and cries out, saying, "This is the One I told you about: 'The One who comes after me is greater than I am, because he was living before me.' "

16 Because he was full of grace and truth, from him we all received one gift after another. 17 The law was given through Moses, but grace and truth came through Jesus Christ. 18 No one has ever seen God. But God the only Son is very close to the Father, and he has shown us what God is like.[12]

---

[12] New Century Version (NCV)

Finding Ancient Wisdom for Discovery

section three
Jesus' life

passage

Jesus is baptized

John 1:19-34

19 Here is the truth John told when the leaders in Jerusalem sent priests and Levites to ask him, "Who are you?"

20 John spoke freely and did not refuse to answer. He said, "I am not the Christ."

21 So they asked him, "Then who are you? Are you Elijah?"

He answered, "No, I am not."

"Are you the Prophet?" they asked.

He answered, "No."

22 Then they said, "Who are you? Give us an answer to tell those who sent us. What do you say about yourself?"

23 John told them in the words of the prophet Isaiah:

"I am the voice of one calling out in the desert:

'Make the road straight for the Lord.' "

24 Some Pharisees who had been sent asked John:

25 "If you are not the Christ or Elijah or the Prophet, why do you baptize people?"

26 John answered, "I baptize with water, but there is one here with you that you don't know about.

27 He is the One who comes after me. I am not good enough to untie the strings of his sandals."

28 This all happened at Bethany on the other side of the Jordan River, where John was baptizing people.

29 The next day John saw Jesus coming toward him. John said, "Look, the Lamb of God, who takes away the sin of the world! 30 This is the One I was talking about when I said, 'A man will come after me, but he is greater than I am, because he was living before me.' 31 Even I did not know who he was, although I came baptizing with water so that the people of Israel would know who he is."

32-33 Then John said, "I saw the Spirit come down from heaven in the form of a dove and rest on him. Until then I did not know who the Christ was. But the God who sent me to baptize with water told me, 'You will see the Spirit come down and rest on a man; he is the One who will baptize with the Holy Spirit.'

34 I have seen this happen, and I tell you the truth: This man is the Son of God."[13]

---

[13] New Century Version (NCV)

passage

the testing of Jesus

Matthew 4:1-22

1 The Spirit then led Jesus into the desert to be tempted by the devil. 2 Jesus fasted for 40 days and 40 nights. After this fast, He was, *as you can imagine,* hungry. 3 *But He was also curiously stronger,* when the tempter came to Jesus.

Devil: If You are the Son of God, tell these stones to become bread.

Jesus *(quoting Deuteronomy)*: 4 It is written, "Man does not live by bread alone. Rather, he lives on every word that comes from the mouth of the Eternal One."

5 Then the devil took Jesus to the holy city, *Jerusalem,* and he had Jesus stand at the very highest point in the holy temple.

Devil: 6 If You are the Son of God, jump! *And then we will see if You fulfill* the Scripture that says, He will command His heavenly messengers concerning You, and the messengers will buoy You in their hands so that You will not *crash, or fall, or even* graze Your foot on a stone.

Jesus: 7 That is not the only thing Scripture says. It also says, "Do not put the Eternal One, your God, to the test."

8 And still the devil *subjected Jesus to a third test. He* took Jesus to the top of a very high mountain, and he showed Jesus all the kingdoms of the world in all their

splendor and glory, *their power and pomp.*

Devil: 9 If You bow down and worship me, I will give You all these kingdoms.

Jesus: 10 Get away from Me, Satan. *I will not serve you. I will instead follow* Scripture, which tells us to "worship the Eternal One, your God, and serve only Him."

11 Then the devil left Jesus. And heavenly messengers came and ministered to Him.

12 *It was not long until powerful people put* John in prison. When Jesus learned this, He went back to Galilee. 13 He moved from Nazareth to Capernaum, a town by the sea in the regions of Zebulun and Naphtali. 14 He did this to fulfill one of the prophecies of Isaiah:

15 In the land of Zebulun and the land of Naphtali, the road to the sea along the Jordan in Galilee, the land of the outsiders—

16 *In these places*, the people who had been living in darkness saw a great light. The light of life will overtake those who dwelt in the shadowy darkness of death.

17 From that time on, preaching was part of Jesus' work.

Jesus: Repent, for the kingdom of heaven is at hand.

18 *One day* Jesus was walking along the Sea of Galilee when He saw Simon (also called Peter) and Andrew

throwing their nets into the water. They were, of course, fishermen.

Jesus: 19 *Come*, follow Me, and I will make you fishers of men.

20 Immediately Peter and Andrew left their fishnets and followed Jesus.

21 Going on from there, Jesus saw two more brothers, James the son of Zebedee and his brother John. *They, too, were fishermen.* They were in a boat with their father Zebedee getting their nets ready to fish. Jesus summoned them, *just as He had called to Peter and Andrew*, 22 and immediately they left their boat and their father to follow Jesus.[14]

---

[14] The Voice

passage

Jesus meets the Samaritan *woman*

John 4:1-26, 39-42

1 Jesus knew that the Pharisees had heard that he was winning and baptizing more followers than John was. 2 But Jesus' disciples were really the ones doing the baptizing, and not Jesus himself. 3 Jesus left Judea and started for Galilee again.

4 This time he had to go through Samaria, 5 and on his way he came to the town of Sychar. It was near the field that Jacob had long ago given to his son Joseph. 6-8 The well that Jacob had dug was still there, and Jesus sat down beside it because he was tired from traveling. It was noon, and after Jesus' disciples had gone into town to buy some food, a Samaritan woman came to draw water from the well.

Jesus asked her, "Would you please give me a drink of water?"

9 "You are a Jew," she replied, "and I am a Samaritan woman. How can you ask me for a drink of water when Jews and Samaritans won't have anything to do with each other?"

10 Jesus answered, "You don't know what God wants to give you, and you don't know who is asking you for a drink. If you did, you would ask me for the water that gives life."

11 "Sir," the woman said, "you don't even have a bucket, and the well is deep. Where are you going to

get this life-giving water? 12 Our ancestor Jacob dug this well for us, and his family and animals got water from it. Are you greater than Jacob?"

13 Jesus answered, "Everyone who drinks this water will get thirsty again. 14 But no one who drinks the water I give will ever be thirsty again. The water I give will become in that person a flowing fountain that gives eternal life."

15 The woman replied, "Sir, please give me a drink of that water! Then I won't get thirsty and have to come to this well again."

16 Jesus told her, "Go and bring your husband."

17-18 The woman answered, "I don't have a husband." "That's right," Jesus replied, "you're telling the truth. You don't have a husband. You have already been married five times, and the man you are now living with isn't your husband."

19 The woman said, "Sir, I can see that you are a prophet.

20 My ancestors worshiped on this mountain, but you Jews say Jerusalem is the only place to worship."

21 Jesus said to her: Believe me, the time is coming when you won't worship the Father either on this mountain or in Jerusalem. 22 You Samaritans don't really know the one you worship. But we Jews do know the God we worship, and by using us, God will save the world.

23 But a time is coming, and it is already here! Even now the true worshipers are being led by the Spirit to worship the Father according to the truth. These are the ones the Father is seeking to worship him.

24 God is Spirit, and those who worship God must be led by the Spirit to worship him according to the truth. 25 The woman said, "I know that the Messiah will come. He is the one we call Christ. When he comes, he will explain everything to us."

26 "I am that one," Jesus told her, "and I am speaking to you now."

39 A lot of Samaritans in that town put their faith in Jesus because the woman had said, "This man told me everything I have ever done." 40 They came and asked him to stay in their town, and he stayed on for two days. 41 Many more Samaritans put their faith in Jesus because of what they heard him say. 42 They told the woman, "We no longer have faith in Jesus just because of what you told us. We have heard him ourselves, and we are certain that he is the Savior of the world!"[15]

---

[15] Contemporary English Version (CEV)

passage

Jesus' authority over spirits

Mark 5:1-20

1 So they arrived at the other side of the lake, in the region of the Gerasenes. 2 When Jesus climbed out of the boat, a man possessed by an evil spirit came out from the tombs to meet him. 3 This man lived in the burial caves and could no longer be restrained, even with a chain. 4 Whenever he was put into chains and shackles—as he often was—he snapped the chains from his wrists and smashed the shackles. No one was strong enough to subdue him. 5 Day and night he wandered among the burial caves and in the hills, howling and cutting himself with sharp stones.

6 When Jesus was still some distance away, the man saw him, ran to meet him, and bowed low before him. 7 With a shriek, he screamed, "Why are you interfering with me, Jesus, Son of the Most High God? In the name of God, I beg you, don't torture me!"

8 For Jesus had already said to the spirit, "Come out of the man, you evil spirit."

9 Then Jesus demanded, "What is your name?"

And he replied, "My name is Legion, because there are many of us inside this man." 10 Then the evil spirits begged him again and again not to send them to some distant place.

11 There happened to be a large herd of pigs feeding on the hillside nearby. 12 "Send us into those pigs,"

the spirits begged. "Let us enter them."

13 So Jesus gave them permission. The evil spirits came out of the man and entered the pigs, and the entire herd of about 2,000 pigs plunged down the steep hillside into the lake and drowned in the water.

14 The herdsmen fled to the nearby town and the surrounding countryside, spreading the news as they ran. People rushed out to see what had happened.

15 A crowd soon gathered around Jesus, and they saw the man who had been possessed by the legion of demons. He was sitting there fully clothed and perfectly sane, and they were all afraid. 16 Then those who had seen what happened told the others about the demon-possessed man and the pigs. 17 And the crowd began pleading with Jesus to go away and leave them alone.

18 As Jesus was getting into the boat, the man who had been demon possessed begged to go with him.

19 But Jesus said, "No, go home to your family, and tell them everything the Lord has done for you and how merciful he has been." 20 So the man started off to visit the Ten Towns of that region and began to proclaim the great things Jesus had done for him; and everyone was amazed at what he told them.[16]

---

[16] New Living Translation (NLT)

passage

death and burial of Jesus

John 19:28-42

28 After this, Jesus knew that everything had been done. So that the Scripture would come true, he said, "I am thirsty." 29 There was a jar full of vinegar there, so the soldiers soaked a sponge in it, put the sponge on a branch of a hyssop plant, and lifted it to Jesus' mouth. 30 When Jesus tasted the vinegar, he said, "It is finished." Then he bowed his head and died.

31 This day was Preparation Day, and the next day was a special Sabbath day. Since the religious leaders did not want the bodies to stay on the cross on the Sabbath day, they asked Pilate to order that the legs of the men be broken and the bodies be taken away.

32 So the soldiers came and broke the legs of the first man on the cross beside Jesus. Then they broke the legs of the man on the other cross beside Jesus.

33 But when the soldiers came to Jesus and saw that he was already dead, they did not break his legs.

34 But one of the soldiers stuck his spear into Jesus' side, and at once blood and water came out.

35 (The one who saw this happen is the one who told us this, and whatever he says is true. And he knows that he tells the truth, and he tells it so that you might believe.) 36 These things happened to make the

Scripture come true: "Not one of his bones will be broken." 37 And another Scripture says, "They will look at the one they stabbed."

38 Later, Joseph from Arimathea asked Pilate if he could take the body of Jesus. (Joseph was a secret follower of Jesus, because he was afraid of some of the leaders.) Pilate gave his permission, so Joseph came and took Jesus' body away.

39 Nicodemus, who earlier had come to Jesus at night, went with Joseph. He brought about seventy-five pounds of myrrh and aloes. 40 These two men took Jesus' body and wrapped it with the spices in pieces of linen cloth, which is how they bury the dead. 41 In the place where Jesus was crucified, there was a garden. In the garden was a new tomb that had never been used before. 42 The men laid Jesus in that tomb because it was nearby, and they were preparing to start their Sabbath day.[17]

---

[17] New Century Version (NCV)

passage

Jesus meets followers after rising again

Luke 24:13-35

13 *Picture this:* That same day, two other disciples *(not of the eleven)* are traveling the seven miles from Jerusalem to Emmaus. 14 As they walk along, they talk back and forth about all that has transpired during recent days.

15 While they're talking, discussing, and conversing, Jesus catches up to them and begins walking with them, 16 but for some reason they don't recognize Him.

Jesus: 17 *You two seem deeply engrossed in conversation. What are you talking about as you walk along this road?*

They stop walking and just stand there, looking sad. 18 One of them—Cleopas is his name—speaks up.

Cleopas: You must be the only visitor in Jerusalem who hasn't heard about what's been going on over the last few days.

Jesus: 19 What are you talking about?

Two Disciples: It's all about the man named Jesus of Nazareth. He was a mighty prophet who did amazing miracles and preached powerful messages in the sight of God and everyone around. 20 Our chief priests and authorities handed Him over to be executed—crucified, in fact. 21 We had been hoping that He was the One—you know, the One who would liberate all

Israel *and bring God's promises*. Anyway, on top of all this, just this morning—the third day after the execution—22 some women in our group really shocked us. They went to the tomb early this morning, 23 but they didn't see His body anywhere. Then they came back and told us they did see something— a vision of heavenly messengers—and these messengers said that Jesus was alive. 24 Some people in our group went to the tomb to check it out, and just as the women had said, it was empty. But they didn't see Jesus.

Jesus: 25 Come on, men! Why are you being so foolish? Why are your hearts so sluggish when it comes to believing what the prophets have been saying all along? 26 Didn't it have to be this way? Didn't the Anointed One have to experience these sufferings in order to come into His glory?

27 Then He begins with Moses and continues, prophet by prophet, explaining the meaning of the Hebrew Scriptures, showing how they were talking about the very things that had happened to Jesus.

28 About this time, they are nearing their destination. Jesus keeps walking ahead as if He has no plans to stop there, 29 but they convince Him to join them.

Two Disciples: Please, be our guest. It's getting late, and soon it will be too dark to walk.

So He accompanies them to their home. 30 When they sit down at the table for dinner, He takes the bread in His hands, He gives thanks for it, and then He breaks it and hands it to them. 31 At that instant, *two things happen simultaneously:* their eyes are suddenly opened so they recognize Him, and He instantly vanishes—just disappears before their eyes.

Two Disciples *(to each other)*: 32 *Amazing!* Weren't our hearts on fire within us while He was talking to us on the road? *Didn't you feel it all coming clear* as He explained the meaning of the Hebrew Scriptures?

33 So they get up immediately and rush back to Jerusalem—*all seven miles*—where they find the eleven gathered together—the eleven plus a number of others. 34 *Before Cleopas and his companion can tell their story,* the others have their own story to tell.

Other Disciples: The Lord has risen indeed! It's true! He appeared to Simon!

35 Then the two men report their own experience—their conversation along the road, their moment of realization and recognition as He broke the bread.[18]

---

[18] The Voice

Finding Ancient Wisdom for Discovery

section four
God Makes a Way

passage

God creates people

Genesis 2:4-24

4 That's how God created the heavens and the earth. When the Lord God made the heavens and the earth,

5 no grass or plants were growing anywhere. God had not yet sent any rain, and there was no one to work the land. 6 But streams came up from the ground and watered the earth.

7 The Lord God took some soil from the ground and made a man. God breathed life into the man, and the man started breathing. 8 The Lord made a garden in a place called Eden, which was in the east, and he put the man there.

9 The Lord God filled the garden with all kinds of beautiful trees and fruit trees. Two other trees were in the middle of the garden. One of these gave life—the other gave the wisdom to know the difference between right and wrong.

10 From Eden a river flowed out to water the garden, then it divided into four rivers. 11 The first one is the Pishon River that flows through the land of Havilah, 12 where pure gold, rare perfumes, and precious stones are found. 13 The second is the Gihon River that winds through Ethiopia. 14 The Tigris River that flows east of Assyria is the third, and the fourth is the Euphrates River.

15 The Lord God put the man in the Garden of Eden to take care of it and to look after it.

16 But the Lord told him, "You may eat fruit from any tree in the garden, 17 except the one that has the power to let you know the difference between right

and wrong. If you eat any fruit from that tree, you will die before the day is over!"

18 The Lord God said, "It isn't good for the man to live alone. I will make a suitable partner for him."

19-20 So the Lord took some soil and made animals and birds. He brought them to the man to see what names he would give each of them. Then the man named the tame animals and the birds and the wild animals. That's how they got their names. None of these was the right kind of partner for the man.

21 So the Lord God made him fall into a deep sleep, and he took out one of the man's ribs. Then after closing the man's side, 22 the Lord made a woman out of the rib. The Lord God brought her to the man,

23 and the man exclaimed, "Here is someone like me! She is part of my body, my own flesh and bones. She came from me, a man. So I will name her Woman!"

24 That's why a man will leave his own father and mother. He marries a woman, and the two of them become like one person.[19]

---

[19] Contemporary English Version (CEV)

passage

God judges his creation

Genesis 6:5-22, 7:17-24, 8:18-22

5 The Lord observed the extent of human wickedness on the earth, and he saw that everything they thought or imagined was consistently and totally evil.

6 So the Lord was sorry he had ever made them and put them on the earth. It broke his heart.

7 And the Lord said, "I will wipe this human race I have created from the face of the earth. Yes, and I will destroy every living thing—all the people, the large animals, the small animals that scurry along the ground, and even the birds of the sky. I am sorry I ever made them." 8 But Noah found favor with the Lord.

9 This is the account of Noah and his family. Noah was a righteous man, the only blameless person living on earth at the time, and he walked in close fellowship with God. 10 Noah was the father of three sons: Shem, Ham, and Japheth.

11 Now God saw that the earth had become corrupt and was filled with violence. 12 God observed all this corruption in the world, for everyone on earth was corrupt. 13 So God said to Noah, "I have decided to destroy all living creatures, for they have filled the earth with violence. Yes, I will wipe them all out along with the earth!

14 "Build a large boat from cypress wood and waterproof it with tar, inside and out. Then construct decks and stalls throughout its interior.

15 Make the boat 450 feet long, 75 feet wide, and 45 feet high. 16 Leave an 18-inch opening below the roof all the way around the boat. Put the door on the side, and build three decks inside the boat—lower, middle, and upper.

17 "Look! I am about to cover the earth with a flood that will destroy every living thing that breathes. Everything on earth will die. 18 But I will confirm my covenant with you. So enter the boat—you and your wife and your sons and their wives. 19 Bring a pair of every kind of animal—a male and a female—into the boat with you to keep them alive during the flood.

20 Pairs of every kind of bird, and every kind of animal, and every kind of small animal that scurries along the ground, will come to you to be kept alive.

21 And be sure to take on board enough food for your family and for all the animals."

22 So Noah did everything exactly as God had commanded him.

17 For forty days the floodwaters grew deeper, covering the ground and lifting the boat high above the earth. 18 As the waters rose higher and higher above the ground, the boat floated safely on the surface. 19 Finally, the water covered even the highest mountains on the earth, 20 rising more than twenty-two feet above the highest peaks. 21 All the living things on earth died—birds, domestic animals, wild animals, small animals that scurry along the ground, and all the people. 22 Everything that breathed and lived on dry land died. 23 God wiped out every living thing on the earth—people, livestock, small animals

that scurry along the ground, and the birds of the sky. All were destroyed. The only people who survived were Noah and those with him in the boat. 24 And the floodwaters covered the earth for 150 days.

18 So Noah, his wife, and his sons and their wives left the boat. 19 And all of the large and small animals and birds came out of the boat, pair by pair.
20 Then Noah built an altar to the Lord, and there he sacrificed as burnt offerings the animals and birds that had been approved for that purpose.
21 And the Lord was pleased with the aroma of the sacrifice and said to himself, "I will never again curse the ground because of the human race, even though everything they think or imagine is bent toward evil from childhood. I will never again destroy all living things. 22 As long as the earth remains, there will be planting and harvest, cold and heat, summer and winter, day and night."[20]

.

---

[20] New Living Translation (NLT)

passage

*God makes promises
to all creation*

Genesis 9:1-19

1 Then God blessed Noah and his sons and said to them, "Have many children; grow in number and fill the earth. 2 Every animal on earth, every bird in the sky, every animal that crawls on the ground, and every fish in the sea will respect and fear you. I have given them to you.

3 "Everything that moves, everything that is alive, is yours for food. Earlier I gave you the green plants, but now I give you everything for food. 4 But you must not eat meat that still has blood in it, because blood gives life. 5 I will demand blood for life. I will demand the life of any animal that kills a person, and I will demand the life of anyone who takes another person's life.

6 "Whoever kills a human being will be killed by a human being, because God made humans in his own image.

7 "As for you, Noah, I want you and your family to have many children, to grow in number on the earth, and to become many."

8 Then God said to Noah and his sons, 9 "Now I am making my agreement with you and your people who will live after you, 10 and with every living thing that is with you—the birds, the tame and the wild animals, and with everything that came out of the boat with you—with every living thing on earth. 11 I make this agreement with you: I will never again destroy all living things by a flood. A flood will never again destroy the earth."

12 And God said, "This is the sign of the agreement between me and you and every living creature that is with you. 13 I am putting my rainbow in the clouds as the sign of the agreement between me and the earth. 14 When I bring clouds over the earth and a rainbow appears in them, 15 I will remember my agreement between me and you and every living thing. Floods will never again destroy all life on the earth. 16 When the rainbow appears in the clouds, I will see it and I will remember the agreement that continues forever between me and every living thing on the earth."

17 So God said to Noah, "The rainbow is a sign of the agreement that I made with all living things on earth." 18 The sons of Noah who came out of the boat with him were Shem, Ham, and Japheth. (Ham was the father of Canaan.) 19 These three men were Noah's sons, and all the people on earth came from these three sons.[21]

---

[21] New Century Version (NCV)

passage

Abraham's big test

Genesis 21:1-6, 22:1-19

1 The Lord was good to Sarah and kept his promise.
2 Although Abraham was very old, Sarah had a son exactly at the time God had said. 3 Abraham named his son Isaac, 4 and when the boy was eight days old, Abraham circumcised him, just as God had commanded. 5 Abraham was 100 years old when Isaac was born, 6 and Sarah said, "God has made me laugh. And now everyone will laugh with me.

1 Some years later God decided to test Abraham, so he spoke to him.
Abraham answered, "Here I am, Lord."
2 The Lord said, "Go get Isaac, your only son, the one you dearly love! Take him to the land of Moriah, and I will show you a mountain where you must sacrifice him to me on the fires of an altar." 3 So Abraham got up early the next morning and chopped wood for the fire. He put a saddle on his donkey and set out with Isaac and two servants for the place where God had told him to go. 4 Three days later Abraham looked off in the distance and saw the place. 5 He told his servants, "Stay here with the donkey, while my son and I go over there to worship. We will come back."
6 Abraham put the wood on Isaac's shoulder, but he carried the hot coals and the knife. As the two of them walked along, 7-8 Isaac said, "Father, we have the coals and the wood, but where is the lamb for the

sacrifice? "My son," Abraham answered, "God will provide the lamb." The two of them walked on, and 9 when they reached the place that God had told him about, Abraham built an altar and placed the wood on it. Next, he tied up his son and put him on the wood. 10 He then took the knife and got ready to kill his son. 11 But the Lord's angel shouted from heaven, "Abraham! Abraham!" "Here I am!" he answered.

12 "Don't hurt the boy or harm him in any way!" the angel said. "Now I know that you truly obey God, because you were willing to offer him your only son."

13 Abraham looked up and saw a ram caught by its horns in the bushes. So he took the ram and sacrificed it instead of his son. 14 Abraham named that place "The Lord Will Provide." And even now people say, "On the mountain of the Lord it will be provided."

15 The Lord's angel called out from heaven a second time: 16 You were willing to offer your only son to the Lord, and so he makes you this solemn promise, 17 "I will bless you and give you such a large family, that someday your descendants will be more numerous than the stars in the sky or the grains of sand along the seashore. They will defeat their enemies and take over the cities where their enemies live. 18 You have obeyed me, and so you and your descendants will be a blessing to all nations on earth."

19 Abraham and Isaac went back to the servants who had come with him, and they returned to Abraham's home in Beersheba.[22]

---

[22] Contemporary English Version (CEV)

passage

God's commands

Deuteronomy 5:1-21, 5:32-6:2

1 Moses called all the people of Israel together and said, "Listen carefully, Israel. Hear the decrees and regulations I am giving you today, so you may learn them and obey them!

2 "The Lord our God made a covenant with us at Mount Sinai. 3 The Lord did not make this covenant with our ancestors, but with all of us who are alive today. 4 At the mountain the Lord spoke to you face to face from the heart of the fire. 5 I stood as an intermediary between you and the Lord, for you were afraid of the fire and did not want to approach the mountain. He spoke to me, and I passed his words on to you. This is what he said:

6 "I am the Lord your God, who rescued you from the land of Egypt, the place of your slavery.

7 "You must not have any other god but me.

8 "You must not make for yourself an idol of any kind, or an image of anything in the heavens or on the earth or in the sea. 9 You must not bow down to them or worship them, for I, the Lord your God, am a jealous God who will not tolerate your affection for any other gods. I lay the sins of the parents upon their children; the entire family is affected—even children in the third and fourth generations of those who reject me. 10 But I lavish unfailing love for a thousand generations on those who love me and obey my commands.

11 "You must not misuse the name of the Lord your God. The Lord will not let you go unpunished if you misuse his name.

12 "Observe the Sabbath day by keeping it holy, as the Lord your God has commanded you. 13 You have six days each week for your ordinary work, 14 but the seventh day is a Sabbath day of rest dedicated to the Lord your God. On that day no one in your household may do any work. This includes you, your sons and daughters, your male and female servants, your oxen and donkeys and other livestock, and any foreigners living among you. All your male and female servants must rest as you do.

15 Remember that you were once slaves in Egypt, but the Lord your God brought you out with his strong hand and powerful arm. That is why the Lord your God has commanded you to rest on the Sabbath day.

16 "Honor your father and mother, as the Lord your God commanded you. Then you will live a long, full life in the land the Lord your God is giving you.

17 "You must not murder.

18 "You must not commit adultery.

19 "You must not steal.

20 "You must not testify falsely against your neighbor.

21 "You must not covet your neighbor's wife. You must not covet your neighbor's house or land, male or female servant, ox or donkey, or anything else that belongs to your neighbor.

32 So Moses told the people, "You must be careful to obey all the commands of the Lord your God, following his instructions in every detail.

33 Stay on the path that the Lord your God has commanded you to follow. Then you will live long and prosperous lives in the land you are about to enter and occupy.

1 "These are the commands, decrees, and regulations that the Lord your God commanded me to teach you. You must obey them in the land you are about to enter and occupy, 2 and you and your children and grandchildren must fear the Lord your God as long as you live. If you obey all his decrees and commands, you will enjoy a long life.[23]

---

[23] New Living Translation (NLT)

passage

God's Word makes us wise

Psalm 19:1-14

1 The heavens declare the glory of God, and the skies announce what his hands have made.

2 Day after day they tell the story; night after night they tell it again. 3 They have no speech or words; they have no voice to be heard. 4 But their message goes out through all the world; their words go everywhere on earth. The sky is like a home for the sun. 5 The sun comes out like a bridegroom from his bedroom. It rejoices like an athlete eager to run a race.

6 The sun rises at one end of the sky and follows its path to the other end. Nothing hides from its heat.

7 The teachings of the Lord are perfect; they give new strength. The rules of the Lord can be trusted; they make plain people wise. 8 The orders of the Lord are right; they make people happy. The commands of the Lord are pure; they light up the way. 9 Respect for the Lord is good; it will last forever. The judgments of the Lord are true; they are completely right.

10 They are worth more than gold, even the purest gold. They are sweeter than honey, even the finest honey. 11 By them your servant is warned.

Keeping them brings great reward. 12 People cannot see their own mistakes. Forgive me for my secret sins.

13 Keep me from the sins of pride; don't let them rule me. Then I can be pure and innocent of the greatest of sins. 14 I hope my words and thoughts please you. Lord, you are my Rock, the one who saves me.[24]

---

[24] New Century Version (NCV)

Finding Ancient Wisdom for Discovery

section five
Jesus is the Way

passage

man's special relationship with God

Psalm 139:1-18

1 You have looked deep into my heart, Lord, and you know all about me.

2 You know when I am resting or when I am working, and from heaven you discover my thoughts.

3 You notice everything I do and everywhere I go.

4 Before I even speak a word, you know what I will say, 5 and with your powerful arm you protect me from every side.

6 I can't understand all of this! Such wonderful knowledge is far above me. 7 Where could I go to escape from your Spirit or from your sight?

8 If I were to climb up to the highest heavens, you would be there. If I were to dig down to the world of the dead you would also be there. 9 Suppose I had wings like the dawning day and flew across the ocean. 10 Even then your powerful arm would guide and protect me. 11 Or suppose I said, "I'll hide in the dark until night comes to cover me over."

12 But you see in the dark because daylight and dark are all the same to you. 13 You are the one who put me together inside my mother's body, 14 and I praise you because of the wonderful way you created me. Everything you do is marvelous! Of this I have no doubt.

15 Nothing about me is hidden from you! I was secretly woven together out of human sight,

16 but with your own eyes you saw my body being formed. Even before I was born, you had written in your book everything about me. 17 Your thoughts are far beyond my understanding, much more than I could ever imagine.

18 I try to count your thoughts, but they outnumber the grains of sand on the beach. And when I awake, I will find you nearby.[25]

---

[25] Contemporary English Version (CEV)

passage

*all have turned away
from God*

Psalms 14:1-7
53:1-6

1 Only fools say in their hearts, "There is no God." They are corrupt, and their actions are evil; not one of them does good!

2 The Lord looks down from heaven on the entire human race; he looks to see if anyone is truly wise, if anyone seeks God.

3 But no, all have turned away; all have become corrupt. No one does good, not a single one!

4 Will those who do evil never learn? They eat up my people like bread and wouldn't think of praying to the Lord. 5 Terror will grip them, for God is with those who obey him.

6 The wicked frustrate the plans of the oppressed, but the Lord will protect his people.

7 Who will come from Mount Zion to rescue Israel? When the Lord restores his people, Jacob will shout with joy, and Israel will rejoice.

1 Only fools say in their hearts, "There is no God." They are corrupt, and their actions are evil; not one of them does good!

2 God looks down from heaven on the entire human race; he looks to see if anyone is truly wise, if anyone seeks God.

3 But no, all have turned away; all have become corrupt. No one does good, not a single one!

4 Will those who do evil never learn? They eat up my people like bread and wouldn't think of praying to God.

5 Terror will grip them, terror like they have never known before. God will scatter the bones of your enemies. You will put them to shame, for God has rejected them.

6 Who will come from Mount Zion to rescue Israel? When God restores his people, Jacob will shout with joy, and Israel will rejoice.[26]

---

[26] New Living Translation (NLT)

passage

sacrifices for sin

Leviticus 4:13-31

13 " 'If the whole nation of Israel sins accidentally without knowing it and does something the Lord has commanded not to be done, they are guilty.

14 When they learn about the sin they have done, they must offer a young bull as a sin offering and bring it before the Meeting Tent. 15 The elders of the group of people must put their hands on the bull's head before the Lord, and it must be killed before the Lord.

16 Then the appointed priest must bring some of the bull's blood into the Meeting Tent. 17 Dipping his finger in the blood, he must sprinkle it seven times before the Lord in front of the curtain. 18 Then he must put some of the blood on the corners of the altar that is before the Lord in the Meeting Tent. The priest must pour out the rest of the blood at the bottom of the altar of burnt offering, which is at the entrance to the Meeting Tent. 19 He must remove all the fat from the animal and burn it on the altar; 20 he will do the same thing with this bull that he did with the first bull of the sin offering. In this way the priest removes the sins of the people so they will belong to the Lord and be forgiven. 21 Then the priest must carry the bull outside the camp and burn it, just as he did with the

first bull. This is the sin offering for the whole community.

22" 'If a ruler sins by accident and does something the Lord his God has commanded must not be done, he is guilty. 23 When he learns about his sin, he must bring a male goat that has nothing wrong with it as his offering. 24 The ruler must put his hand on the goat's head and kill it in the place where they kill the whole burnt offering before the Lord ; it is a sin offering.

25 The priest must take some of the blood of the sin offering on his finger and put it on the corners of the altar of burnt offering. He must pour out the rest of the blood at the bottom of the altar of burnt offering. 26 He must burn all the goat's fat on the altar in the same way he burns the fat of the fellowship offerings. In this way the priest removes the ruler's sin so he belongs to the Lord, and the Lord will forgive him. 27 " 'If any person in the community sins by accident and does something which the Lord has commanded must not be done, he is guilty.

28 When the person learns about his sin, he must bring a female goat that has nothing wrong with it as an offering for his sin. 29 He must put his hand on the animal's head and kill it at the place of the whole burnt offering. 30 Then the priest must take some of the goat's blood on his finger and put it on the corners

of the altar of burnt offering. He must pour out the rest of the goat's blood at the bottom of the altar.

31 Then the priest must remove all the goat's fat in the same way the fat is removed from the fellowship offerings. He must burn it on the altar as a smell pleasing to the Lord. In this way the priest will remove that person's sin so he will belong to the Lord, and the Lord will forgive him.[27]

---

[27] New Century Version (NCV)

passage

how we will know the
Messiah/Christ

Psalm 2:1-12

1 Why do the nations plot, and why do their people make useless plans? 2 The kings of this earth have all joined together to turn against the Lord and his chosen king. 3 They say, "Let's cut the ropes and set ourselves free!" 4 In heaven the Lord laughs as he sits on his throne, making fun of the nations.

5 The Lord becomes furious and threatens them. His anger terrifies them as he says, 6 "I've put my king on Zion, my sacred hill." 7 I will tell the promise that the Lord made to me: "You are my son, because today I have become your father. 8 Ask me for the nations, and every nation on earth will belong to you.

9 You will smash them with an iron rod and shatter them like dishes of clay." 10 Be smart, all you rulers, and pay close attention. 11 Serve and honor the Lord; be glad and tremble. 12 Show respect to his son because if you don't, the Lord might become furious and suddenly destroy you. But he blesses and protects everyone who runs to him.[28]

---

[28] Contemporary English Version (CEV)

passage

Jesus heals a paralyzed man

Luke 5:17-26

17 One day Jesus was teaching *in a house*, and the healing power of the Lord was with Him. Pharisees and religious scholars were sitting and listening, having come from villages all across the regions of Galilee and Judea and from *the holy city of* Jerusalem.

18 Some men came *to the house*, carrying a paralyzed man on his bed pallet. They wanted to bring him in and present him to Jesus, 19 but the house was so packed with people that they couldn't get in. So they climbed up on the roof and pulled off some roof tiles. Then they lowered the man *by ropes* so he came to rest right in front of Jesus.

20 In this way, their faith was visible to Jesus.

Jesus *(to the man on the pallet)*: My friend, all your sins are forgiven.

21 The Pharisees and religious scholars were offended at this. They turned to one another and asked questions.

Pharisees and Religious Scholars: Who does He think He is? Wasn't that blasphemous? Who can pronounce that a person's sins are forgiven? Who but God alone?

Jesus *(responding with His own question)*: 22 Why are your hearts full of questions? 23 Which is easier to say, "Your sins are forgiven" or "Get up and walk"?

24 Just so you'll know that the Son of Man is fully authorized to forgive sins on earth (He turned to the paralyzed fellow *lying on the pallet*), I say, get up, take your mat, and go home.

25 Then, right in front of their eyes, the man stood up, picked up his bed, and left to go home—full of praises for God! 26 Everyone was stunned. They couldn't help but feel awestruck, and they praised God too.

People: We've seen extraordinary things today.[29]

---

[29] The Voice

passage

Jesus shares a last meal

Matthew 26:17-30

17 On the first day of the Festival of Unleavened Bread, the disciples said to Jesus,

Disciples: Where would You like us to prepare the Passover meal for You?

Jesus: 18 Go into the city, find a certain man, and say to him, "The Teacher says, 'My time is near, and I am going to celebrate Passover at your house with My disciples.' " 19 So the disciples *went off,* followed Jesus' instructions, and got the Passover meal ready. 20 When evening came, Jesus sat down with the twelve. 21 And they ate their dinner.

Jesus: I tell you this: one of you here will betray Me.

22 The disciples, *of course,* were horrified. **A Disciple:** Not me!

Another Disciple: *It's not me, Master, is it?*

Jesus: 23 It's the one who shared this dish of food with Me. That is the one who will betray Me. 24 Just as our sacred Scripture has taught, the Son of Man is on His way. But there will be nothing but misery for he who hands Him over. That man will wish he had never been born. 25 At that, Judas, who was indeed planning to betray Him, said,

Judas Iscariot: It's not me, Master, is it? **Jesus:** I believe you've just answered your own question.

26 As they were eating, Jesus took some bread. He offered a blessing *over the bread*, and then He broke it and gave it to His disciples.

Jesus: Take this and eat; it is My body.

27 And then He took the cup *of wine*, He made a blessing over it, and He passed it around the table.

Jesus: Take this and drink, all of you: 28 this is My blood of the new covenant, which is poured out for many for the forgiveness of sins. 29 But I tell you: I will not drink of the fruit of the vine again until I am with you once more, drinking in the kingdom of My Father.

30 *The meal concluded.* Together, all the men sang a hymn *of praise and thanksgiving*, and then they took a late evening walk to the Mount of Olives. [30]

---

[30] The Voice

Finding Ancient Wisdom
for Discovery

section six
Finding Wisdom

passage

to overcome temptation

Luke 4:1-13

1 Jesus, filled with the Holy Spirit, returned from the Jordan River. The Spirit led Jesus into the desert

2 where the devil tempted Jesus for forty days. Jesus ate nothing during that time, and when those days were ended, he was very hungry.

3 The devil said to Jesus, "If you are the Son of God, tell this rock to become bread."

4 Jesus answered, "It is written in the Scriptures: 'A person does not live on bread alone.' "

5 Then the devil took Jesus and showed him all the kingdoms of the world in an instant. 6 The devil said to Jesus, "I will give you all these kingdoms and all their power and glory. It has all been given to me, and I can give it to anyone I wish. 7 If you worship me, then it will all be yours." 8 Jesus answered, "It is written in the Scriptures: 'You must worship the Lord your God and serve only him.' "

9 Then the devil led Jesus to Jerusalem and put him on a high place of the Temple. He said to Jesus, "If you are the Son of God, jump down. 10 It is written in the Scriptures: 'He has put his angels in charge of you to watch over you.'

11 It is also written: 'They will catch you in their hands so that you will not hit your foot on a rock.' "

12 Jesus answered, "But it also says in the Scriptures: 'Do not test the Lord your God.' "

13 After the devil had tempted Jesus in every way, he left him to wait until a better time.[31]

---

[31] New Century Version (NCV)

passage

to find and show love

Matthew 5:38-48

26 A heavenly messenger brought this *short* message from the Lord to Philip *during his time preaching in Samaria:*

Messenger of the Lord: Leave Samaria. Go south to the Jerusalem-Gaza road.

The message was especially unusual because this road runs through the middle of uninhabited desert.

27 But Philip got up, *left the excitement of Samaria,* and did as he was told to do. *Along this road, Philip saw a chariot in the distance. In the chariot was* a dignitary from Ethiopia (the treasurer for Queen Candace), *an African man* who had been castrated. He had gone north to Jerusalem to worship *at the Jewish temple,*

28 and he was now *heading southwest* on his way home. He was seated in the chariot and was reading aloud from a scroll of the prophet Isaiah.

29 Philip received another prompting from the Holy Spirit:

Holy Spirit: Go over to the chariot and climb on board.

30 So he started running until he was even with the chariot. Philip heard the Ethiopian reading aloud and recognized the words from the prophet Isaiah.

Philip: Do you understand the meaning of what you're reading?

The Ethiopian: 31 How can I understand it unless I have a mentor?

Then he invited Philip to sit in the chariot. 32 Here's the passage he was reading from the Hebrew Scriptures: Like a sheep, He was led to be slaughtered. Like a lamb about to be shorn of its wool, He was completely silent.

33 He was humiliated, and He received no justice. Who can describe His peers? *Who would treat Him this way?*

For they snuffed out His life.

The Ethiopian: 34 *Here's my first question.* Is the prophet describing his own situation, or is he describing someone else's *calamity*?

35 That began a conversation in which Philip used the passage to explain the good news of Jesus. 36 Eventually the chariot passed a body of water

beside the road.

The Ethiopian: Since there is water here, is there anything that might prevent me from being ceremonially washed through baptism *and identified as a disciple of Jesus*?

Philip: 37 If you believe in your heart that Jesus the Anointed is God's Son, then nothing can stop you.

The Ethiopian said that he believed.

38 He commanded the charioteer to stop the horses. Then Philip and the Ethiopian official walked together into the water. There Philip baptized him, *initiating him as a fellow disciple*. 39 When they came out of the water, Philip was immediately caught up by the Holy Spirit and taken from the sight of the Ethiopian, who climbed back into his chariot and continued on his journey, overflowing with joy. 40 Philip found himself at a town called Azotus (*formerly the Philistine capital city of Ashdod, on the Mediterranean*); and from there he traveled north again, proclaiming the good news in town after town until he came to Caesarea.[32]

---

[32] The Voice

passage

to <u>not</u> fear circumstances

Luke 8:22-25

22 One day, Jesus and his disciples got into a boat, and he said, "Let's cross the lake." They started out,

23 and while they were sailing across, he went to sleep. Suddenly a storm struck the lake, and the boat started sinking. They were in danger. 24 So they went to Jesus and woke him up, "Master, Master! We are about to drown!" Jesus got up and ordered the wind and waves to stop. They obeyed, and everything was calm. 25 Then Jesus asked the disciples, "Don't you have any faith?" But they were frightened and amazed. They said to each other, "Who is this? He can give orders to the wind and the waves, and they obey him!"[33]

---

[33] Contemporary English Version (CEV)

passage

to forgive and restore

Matthew 18:15-35

15 "If another believer sins against you, go privately and point out the offense. If the other person listens and confesses it, you have won that person back.

16 But if you are unsuccessful, take one or two others with you and go back again, so that everything you say may be confirmed by two or three witnesses.

17 If the person still refuses to listen, take your case to the church. Then if he or she won't accept the church's decision, treat that person as a pagan or a corrupt tax collector.

18 "I tell you the truth, whatever you forbid on earth will be forbidden in heaven, and whatever you permit on earth will be permitted in heaven.

19 "I also tell you this: If two of you agree here on earth concerning anything you ask, my Father in heaven will do it for you. 20 For where two or three gather together as my followers, I am there among them."

21 Then Peter came to him and asked, "Lord, how often should I forgive someone who sins against me? Seven times?"

22 "No, not seven times," Jesus replied, "but seventy times seven!

23 "Therefore, the Kingdom of Heaven can be compared to a king who decided to bring his accounts up to date with servants who had borrowed money from him. 24 In the process, one of his debtors was brought in who owed him millions of dollars.

25 He couldn't pay, so his master ordered that he be sold—along with his wife, his children, and everything he owned—to pay the debt.

26 "But the man fell down before his master and begged him, 'Please, be patient with me, and I will pay it all.' 27 Then his master was filled with pity for him, and he released him and forgave his debt.

28 "But when the man left the king, he went to a fellow servant who owed him a few thousand dollars. He grabbed him by the throat and demanded instant payment.

29 "His fellow servant fell down before him and begged for a little more time. 'Be patient with me, and I will pay it,' he pleaded. 30 But his creditor wouldn't wait. He had the man arrested and put in prison until the debt could be paid in full.

31 "When some of the other servants saw this, they were very upset. They went to the king and told him everything that had happened. 32 Then the king called in the man he had forgiven and said, 'You evil servant! I forgave you that tremendous debt because you pleaded with me. 33 Shouldn't you have mercy on your fellow servant, just as I had mercy on you?'

34 Then the angry king sent the man to prison to be tortured until he had paid his entire debt.

35 "That's what my heavenly Father will do to you if you refuse to forgive your brothers and sisters from your heart."[34]

---

[34] New Living Translation (NLT)

passage

to keep unity in Christ

Ephesians 4:1-6

1 As a prisoner of the Lord, I urge you: Live a life that is worthy of the calling He has *graciously* extended to you. Be humble. 2 Be gentle. Be patient. Tolerate one another in *an atmosphere thick with* love.

3 Make every effort to preserve the unity the Spirit has already created, with peace binding you together.

4 There is one body and one Spirit, just as you were all called to pursue one hope.

5 There is one Lord *Jesus*, one *living* faith, one ceremonial washing through baptism, and

6 one God—the Father over all who is above all, through all, and in all. [35]

---

[35] The Voice

passage

to gain wisdom for living

Psalm 1:1-6

1 Oh, the joys of those who do not follow the advice of the wicked, or stand around with sinners, or join in with mockers.

2 But they delight in the law of the Lord, meditating on it day and night.

3 They are like trees planted along the riverbank, bearing fruit each season. Their leaves never wither, and they prosper in all they do.

4 But not the wicked! They are like worthless chaff, scattered by the wind.

5 They will be condemned at the time of judgment. Sinners will have no place among the godly.

6 For the Lord watches over the path of the godly, but the path of the wicked leads to destruction.[36]

---

[36] New Living Translation (NLT)

Made in the USA
Las Vegas, NV
30 March 2022